50 Ultimate German Bread Recipes for Home

By: Kelly Johnson

Table of Contents

- Bauernbrot (Farmer's Bread)
- Roggenbrot (Rye Bread)
- Vollkornbrot (Whole Grain Bread)
- Pumpernickel
- Brötchen (German Rolls)
- Laugenbrötchen (Pretzel Rolls)
- Laugenstangen (Pretzel Sticks)
- Dinkelbrot (Spelt Bread)
- Kürbiskernbrot (Pumpkin Seed Bread)
- Sonnenblumenkernbrot (Sunflower Seed Bread)
- Mehrkornbrot (Multigrain Bread)
- Schwarzbrot (Black Bread)
- Berliner Landbrot (Berlin Country Bread)
- Krustenbrot (Crusty Bread)
- Zwiebelbrot (Onion Bread)
- Kartoffelbrot (Potato Bread)
- Malzbrot (Malt Bread)
- Fladenbrot (Flatbread)
- Bierbrot (Beer Bread)
- Buttermilchbrot (Buttermilk Bread)
- Leinsamenbrot (Flaxseed Bread)
- Haferbrot (Oat Bread)
- Kastanienbrot (Chestnut Bread)
- Sesambrot (Sesame Bread)
- Rübenbrot (Beet Bread)
- Baguette nach deutscher Art (German-Style Baguette)
- Haferflockenbrot (Oatmeal Bread)
- Speckbrot (Bacon Bread)
- Tomatenbrot (Tomato Bread)
- Kastenbrot (Loaf Bread)
- Gewürzbrot (Spiced Bread)
- Mohnbrot (Poppy Seed Bread)
- Walnussbrot (Walnut Bread)
- Quarkbrot (Quark Bread)
- Chia-Körnerbrot (Chia Seed Bread)

- Sauerteigbrot (Sourdough Bread)
- Dinkelvollkornbrot (Whole Spelt Bread)
- Hefezopf (Yeast Braid Bread)
- Rosinenbrot (Raisin Bread)
- Nussbrot (Nut Bread)
- Müsli-Brot (Muesli Bread)
- Kastanienhonigbrot (Chestnut Honey Bread)
- Apfelbrot (Apple Bread)
- Kürbisbrot (Pumpkin Bread)
- Kirschenbrot (Cherry Bread)
- Vanillebrot (Vanilla Bread)
- Kokosbrot (Coconut Bread)
- Schokoladenbrot (Chocolate Bread)
- Früchtebrot (Fruit Bread)
- Maronenbrot (Marron Bread)

Bauernbrot (Farmer's Bread)

Starter:

- 1 cup (120g) rye flour
- ½ cup (120ml) water
- ¼ teaspoon instant yeast

Dough:

- 2 cups (250g) rye flour
- 2 cups (250g) bread flour
- 1 ½ teaspoons salt
- 1 ½ teaspoons caraway seeds (optional)
- 1 teaspoon instant yeast
- 1 ¼ cups (300ml) warm water
- 1 tablespoon vinegar

Instructions:

1. **Starter:** Mix rye flour, water, and yeast. Cover and ferment for 8-12 hours.
2. **Dough:** Combine flours, salt, caraway seeds, and yeast. Add starter, water, and vinegar. Mix into a shaggy dough.
3. **Knead:** Work dough for 10 minutes until elastic. Cover and rise for 1-2 hours.
4. **Shape:** Form into a round loaf, place on a floured surface, cover, and let rise for 45-60 minutes.
5. **Bake:** Preheat oven to 450°F (230°C) with a tray of hot water. Score the dough, bake for 35-40 minutes until deep brown.
6. **Cool:** Let cool completely on a wire rack before slicing.

Roggenbrot (Rye Bread)

Starter:

- 1 cup (120g) rye flour
- ½ cup (120ml) water
- ¼ teaspoon instant yeast

Dough:

- 3 cups (375g) rye flour
- 1 cup (125g) bread flour
- 1 ½ teaspoons salt
- 1 teaspoon instant yeast
- 1 ½ cups (360ml) warm water
- 1 tablespoon molasses (optional)

Instructions:

1. **Starter:** Mix rye flour, water, and yeast. Cover and ferment for 8-12 hours.
2. **Dough:** Combine flours, salt, and yeast. Add starter, water, and molasses. Mix into a sticky dough.
3. **Knead:** Work dough for 10 minutes. Cover and let rise for 1-2 hours.
4. **Shape:** Form into a loaf, place in a floured basket, and let rise for 45-60 minutes.
5. **Bake:** Preheat oven to 425°F (220°C). Score the top, bake for 40-45 minutes.
6. **Cool:** Let cool completely before slicing.

Vollkornbrot (Whole Grain Bread)

Ingredients:

- 2 cups (250g) whole wheat flour
- 1 cup (120g) rye flour
- ½ cup (75g) sunflower seeds (optional)
- 1 ½ teaspoons salt
- 1 teaspoon instant yeast
- 1 ½ cups (360ml) warm water
- 1 tablespoon honey or molasses

Instructions:

1. **Mix Dough:** Combine flours, seeds, salt, and yeast. Add water and honey, mixing into a sticky dough.
2. **Knead:** Work dough for 10 minutes. Cover and let rise for 1-2 hours.
3. **Shape:** Form into a loaf, place in a greased pan, and let rise for 45-60 minutes.
4. **Bake:** Preheat oven to 400°F (200°C). Bake for 45-50 minutes.
5. **Cool:** Let cool before slicing.

Pumpernickel

Ingredients:

- 2 cups (250g) rye flour
- 1 cup (120g) whole wheat flour
- ½ cup (75g) cracked rye or pumpernickel meal
- 1 teaspoon salt
- 1 teaspoon instant yeast
- 1 ½ cups (360ml) warm water
- 1 tablespoon molasses
- 1 tablespoon cocoa powder (for color and depth)

Instructions:

1. **Mix Dough:** Combine flours, cracked rye, salt, and yeast. Add water, molasses, and cocoa, mixing into a sticky dough.
2. **Knead:** Work dough for 10 minutes. Cover and let rise for 2 hours.
3. **Shape:** Form into a round loaf, place in a greased pan, and let rise for 1 hour.
4. **Bake:** Preheat oven to 350°F (175°C). Bake for 60-70 minutes.
5. **Cool:** Let cool before slicing.

Brötchen (German Rolls)

Ingredients:

- 3 cups (375g) bread flour
- 1 ½ teaspoons salt
- 1 teaspoon sugar
- 1 teaspoon instant yeast
- 1 cup (240ml) warm water
- 1 tablespoon butter (melted)

Instructions:

1. **Mix Dough:** Combine flour, salt, sugar, and yeast. Add water and butter, kneading into a soft dough.
2. **Knead:** Work dough for 10 minutes. Cover and let rise for 1-2 hours.
3. **Shape:** Divide into 8 pieces, shape into rolls, and place on a baking sheet. Let rise for 30-45 minutes.
4. **Bake:** Preheat oven to 425°F (220°C). Bake for 15-20 minutes until golden brown.
5. **Cool:** Let cool before serving.

Laugenbrötchen (Pretzel Rolls)

Ingredients:

- 3 cups (375g) bread flour
- 1 teaspoon salt
- 1 teaspoon sugar
- 1 teaspoon instant yeast
- 1 cup (240ml) warm water
- 2 tablespoons butter, melted
- 4 cups (1L) water (for boiling)
- ¼ cup (60g) baking soda
- Coarse salt for topping

Instructions:

1. **Mix Dough:** Combine flour, salt, sugar, and yeast. Add water and butter, kneading into a smooth dough.
2. **Knead:** Work dough for 10 minutes. Cover and let rise for 1-2 hours.
3. **Shape:** Divide into 8 rolls and place on a lined baking sheet. Let rise for 30 minutes.
4. **Boil:** Preheat oven to 425°F (220°C). Boil water, add baking soda, and dip each roll for 30 seconds.
5. **Bake:** Sprinkle with coarse salt, bake for 15-20 minutes until deep brown.

Laugenstangen (Pretzel Sticks)

Ingredients:

- Same as Laugenbrötchen

Instructions:

1. **Follow the same process** as Laugenbrötchen but shape dough into **long sticks** instead of rolls.
2. **Boil and bake** as directed.

Dinkelbrot (Spelt Bread)

Ingredients:

- 3 cups (375g) spelt flour
- 1 teaspoon salt
- 1 teaspoon instant yeast
- 1 cup (240ml) warm water
- 1 tablespoon honey

Instructions:

1. **Mix Dough:** Combine all ingredients, kneading into a sticky dough.
2. **Knead:** Work dough for 10 minutes. Cover and let rise for 1-2 hours.
3. **Shape:** Form into a loaf, place in a greased pan, and let rise for 45-60 minutes.
4. **Bake:** Preheat oven to 400°F (200°C). Bake for 40-45 minutes.

Kürbiskernbrot (Pumpkin Seed Bread)

Ingredients:

- 2 cups (250g) whole wheat flour
- 1 cup (125g) rye flour
- ½ cup (75g) pumpkin seeds
- 1 teaspoon salt
- 1 teaspoon instant yeast
- 1 ¼ cups (300ml) warm water

Instructions:

1. **Mix Dough:** Combine dry ingredients. Add water, mix into a dough.
2. **Knead:** Work dough for 10 minutes. Let rise for 1-2 hours.
3. **Shape:** Form into a loaf, place in a pan, and let rise for 45 minutes.
4. **Bake:** Preheat oven to 400°F (200°C). Bake for 45-50 minutes.

Sonnenblumenkernbrot (Sunflower Seed Bread)

Ingredients:

- 2 cups (250g) whole wheat flour
- 1 cup (125g) rye flour
- ½ cup (75g) sunflower seeds
- 1 teaspoon salt
- 1 teaspoon instant yeast
- 1 ¼ cups (300ml) warm water

Instructions:

Same process as Kürbiskernbrot, replacing pumpkin seeds with sunflower seeds.

Mehrkornbrot (Multigrain Bread)

Ingredients:

- 1 ½ cups (190g) whole wheat flour
- 1 cup (125g) rye flour
- ½ cup (75g) oats
- ¼ cup (40g) flaxseeds
- 1 teaspoon salt
- 1 teaspoon instant yeast
- 1 ¼ cups (300ml) warm water

Instructions:

1. **Mix, knead, shape, and bake** as in previous whole-grain bread recipes.

Schwarzbrot (Black Bread)

Ingredients:

- 2 cups (250g) rye flour
- 1 cup (125g) whole wheat flour
- ½ cup (120ml) molasses
- 1 teaspoon salt
- 1 teaspoon instant yeast
- 1 ½ cups (360ml) warm water

Instructions:

1. **Mix Dough:** Combine dry ingredients. Add molasses and water, mixing into a sticky dough.
2. **Knead:** Work dough for 10 minutes. Let rise for 2 hours.
3. **Shape:** Place in a greased loaf pan, let rise for 1 hour.
4. **Bake:** Preheat oven to 350°F (175°C). Bake for 60-70 minutes.

Berliner Landbrot (Berlin Country Bread)

Ingredients:

- 2 cups (250g) rye flour
- 2 cups (250g) bread flour
- 1 teaspoon salt
- 1 teaspoon instant yeast
- 1 ¼ cups (300ml) warm water

Instructions:

1. **Mix Dough:** Combine all ingredients, kneading into a smooth dough.
2. **Knead:** Work dough for 10 minutes. Let rise for 1-2 hours.
3. **Shape:** Form into a loaf, let rise for 45-60 minutes.
4. **Bake:** Preheat oven to 450°F (230°C). Bake for 35-40 minutes.

Krustenbrot (Crusty Bread)

Ingredients:

- 3 cups (375g) bread flour
- 1 teaspoon salt
- 1 teaspoon instant yeast
- 1 ¼ cups (300ml) warm water

Instructions:

1. **Mix Dough:** Combine all ingredients, kneading into a smooth dough.
2. **Knead:** Work dough for 10 minutes. Let rise for 1-2 hours.
3. **Shape:** Form into a loaf, place in a Dutch oven, and let rise for 45 minutes.
4. **Bake:** Preheat oven to 450°F (230°C). Bake for 40-45 minutes with the lid on, then 10 minutes uncovered.

Zwiebelbrot (Onion Bread)

Ingredients:

- 3 cups (375g) bread flour
- 1 teaspoon salt
- 1 teaspoon instant yeast
- 1 cup (240ml) warm water
- 1 medium onion, finely chopped and sautéed

Instructions:

1. **Prepare Onions:** Sauté chopped onion in a little butter until golden. Let cool.
2. **Mix Dough:** Combine flour, salt, yeast, and onions. Add warm water, kneading into a smooth dough.
3. **Knead:** Work dough for 10 minutes. Let rise for 1-2 hours.
4. **Shape:** Form into a loaf, let rise for 45 minutes.
5. **Bake:** Preheat oven to 400°F (200°C). Bake for 35-40 minutes.

Kartoffelbrot (Potato Bread)

Ingredients:

- 2 cups (250g) bread flour
- 1 cup (250g) mashed potatoes
- 1 teaspoon salt
- 1 teaspoon instant yeast
- ½ cup (120ml) warm water
- 1 tablespoon butter, melted

Instructions:

1. **Mix Dough:** Combine flour, salt, and yeast. Add mashed potatoes, water, and butter, mixing into a soft dough.
2. **Knead:** Work dough for 10 minutes. Let rise for 1-2 hours.
3. **Shape:** Form into a loaf, let rise for 45 minutes.
4. **Bake:** Preheat oven to 400°F (200°C). Bake for 40-45 minutes.

Malzbrot (Malt Bread)

Ingredients:

- 2 cups (250g) whole wheat flour
- 1 cup (125g) rye flour
- 2 tablespoons malt syrup
- 1 teaspoon salt
- 1 teaspoon instant yeast
- 1 ¼ cups (300ml) warm water

Instructions:

1. **Mix Dough:** Combine dry ingredients. Add malt syrup and water, mixing into a sticky dough.
2. **Knead:** Work dough for 10 minutes. Let rise for 2 hours.
3. **Shape:** Form into a loaf, let rise for 45-60 minutes.
4. **Bake:** Preheat oven to 375°F (190°C). Bake for 40-45 minutes.

Fladenbrot (Flatbread)

Ingredients:

- 3 cups (375g) bread flour
- 1 teaspoon salt
- 1 teaspoon sugar
- 1 teaspoon instant yeast
- 1 cup (240ml) warm water

Instructions:

1. **Mix Dough:** Combine all ingredients, kneading into a soft dough.
2. **Knead:** Work dough for 10 minutes. Let rise for 1 hour.
3. **Shape:** Roll into a large circle or oval, place on a baking sheet, and let rise for 30 minutes.
4. **Bake:** Preheat oven to 425°F (220°C). Bake for 15-20 minutes.

Bierbrot (Beer Bread)

Ingredients:

- 3 cups (375g) bread flour
- 1 teaspoon salt
- 1 teaspoon baking powder
- 1 teaspoon sugar
- 1 ½ cups (360ml) beer

Instructions:

1. **Mix Dough:** Combine all ingredients, mixing into a sticky batter.
2. **Shape:** Pour into a greased loaf pan.
3. **Bake:** Preheat oven to 375°F (190°C). Bake for 45-50 minutes.

Buttermilchbrot (Buttermilk Bread)

Ingredients:

- 3 cups (375g) bread flour
- 1 teaspoon salt
- 1 teaspoon instant yeast
- 1 cup (240ml) warm buttermilk

Instructions:

1. **Mix Dough:** Combine all ingredients, kneading into a smooth dough.
2. **Knead:** Work dough for 10 minutes. Let rise for 1-2 hours.
3. **Shape:** Form into a loaf, let rise for 45-60 minutes.
4. **Bake:** Preheat oven to 400°F (200°C). Bake for 40-45 minutes.

Leinsamenbrot (Flaxseed Bread)

Ingredients:

- 2 cups (250g) whole wheat flour
- 1 cup (125g) rye flour
- ½ cup (75g) flaxseeds
- 1 teaspoon salt
- 1 teaspoon instant yeast
- 1 ¼ cups (300ml) warm water

Instructions:

Same process as Buttermilchbrot, incorporating flaxseeds.

Haferbrot (Oat Bread)

Ingredients:

- 2 cups (250g) whole wheat flour
- 1 cup (125g) bread flour
- ½ cup (75g) rolled oats
- 1 teaspoon salt
- 1 teaspoon instant yeast
- 1 ¼ cups (300ml) warm water

Instructions:

Same process as Buttermilchbrot, incorporating oats.

Kastanienbrot (Chestnut Bread)

Ingredients:

- 2 cups (250g) bread flour
- 1 cup (150g) chestnut flour
- 1 teaspoon salt
- 1 teaspoon instant yeast
- 1 cup (240ml) warm water

Instructions:

Same process as Buttermilchbrot, using chestnut flour.

Sesambrot (Sesame Bread)

Ingredients:

- 3 cups (375g) bread flour
- 1 teaspoon salt
- 1 teaspoon instant yeast
- 1 cup (240ml) warm water
- 2 tablespoons sesame seeds

Instructions:

1. **Mix Dough:** Combine all ingredients, kneading into a soft dough.
2. **Knead:** Work dough for 10 minutes. Let rise for 1-2 hours.
3. **Shape:** Form into a loaf, brush with water, and sprinkle sesame seeds.
4. **Bake:** Preheat oven to 400°F (200°C). Bake for 40-45 minutes.

Rübenbrot (Beet Bread)

Ingredients:

- 2 cups (250g) whole wheat flour
- 1 cup (125g) bread flour
- 1 cup (250g) grated beets
- 1 teaspoon salt
- 1 teaspoon instant yeast
- 1 cup (240ml) warm water

Instructions:

Same process as Buttermilchbrot, incorporating beets.

Baguette nach deutscher Art (German-Style Baguette)

Ingredients:

- 3 cups (375g) bread flour
- 1 teaspoon salt
- 1 teaspoon instant yeast
- 1 cup (240ml) warm water

Instructions:

1. **Mix Dough:** Combine all ingredients, kneading into a smooth dough.
2. **Knead:** Work dough for 10 minutes. Let rise for 1-2 hours.
3. **Shape:** Divide into 2 long baguette shapes and place on a baking sheet. Let rise for 30 minutes.
4. **Bake:** Preheat oven to 450°F (230°C). Bake for 20-25 minutes.

Haferflockenbrot (Oatmeal Bread)

Ingredients:

- 2 cups (250g) whole wheat flour
- 1 cup (125g) bread flour
- ½ cup (75g) rolled oats
- 1 teaspoon salt
- 1 teaspoon instant yeast
- 1 ¼ cups (300ml) warm water

Instructions:

1. **Mix Dough:** Combine all ingredients, kneading into a soft dough.
2. **Knead:** Work dough for 10 minutes. Let rise for 1-2 hours.
3. **Shape:** Form into a loaf, sprinkle with oats, and let rise for 45 minutes.
4. **Bake:** Preheat oven to 400°F (200°C). Bake for 40-45 minutes.

Speckbrot (Bacon Bread)

Ingredients:

- 3 cups (375g) bread flour
- 1 teaspoon salt
- 1 teaspoon instant yeast
- 1 cup (240ml) warm water
- ½ cup (100g) cooked bacon, chopped

Instructions:

1. **Mix Dough:** Combine flour, salt, and yeast. Add water and mix into a soft dough.
2. **Knead:** Work dough for 10 minutes, incorporating bacon. Let rise for 1-2 hours.
3. **Shape:** Form into a loaf, let rise for 45 minutes.
4. **Bake:** Preheat oven to 400°F (200°C). Bake for 40-45 minutes.

Tomatenbrot (Tomato Bread)

Ingredients:

- 2 cups (250g) bread flour
- 1 cup (250g) tomato purée
- 1 teaspoon salt
- 1 teaspoon instant yeast
- ½ teaspoon dried oregano

Instructions:

1. **Mix Dough:** Combine all ingredients, kneading into a soft dough.
2. **Knead:** Work dough for 10 minutes. Let rise for 1-2 hours.
3. **Shape:** Form into a loaf, let rise for 45 minutes.
4. **Bake:** Preheat oven to 375°F (190°C). Bake for 40-45 minutes.

Kastenbrot (Loaf Bread)

Ingredients:

- 3 cups (375g) bread flour
- 1 teaspoon salt
- 1 teaspoon instant yeast
- 1 cup (240ml) warm water

Instructions:

1. **Mix Dough:** Combine all ingredients, kneading into a smooth dough.
2. **Knead:** Work dough for 10 minutes. Let rise for 1-2 hours.
3. **Shape:** Place in a greased loaf pan, let rise for 45 minutes.
4. **Bake:** Preheat oven to 400°F (200°C). Bake for 40-45 minutes.

Gewürzbrot (Spiced Bread)

Ingredients:

- 2 cups (250g) rye flour
- 1 cup (125g) whole wheat flour
- 1 teaspoon salt
- 1 teaspoon instant yeast
- 1 teaspoon caraway seeds
- ½ teaspoon coriander
- ½ teaspoon fennel seeds
- 1 ¼ cups (300ml) warm water

Instructions:

Same as Kastenbrot, incorporating spices.

Mohnbrot (Poppy Seed Bread)

Ingredients:

- 3 cups (375g) bread flour
- 1 teaspoon salt
- 1 teaspoon instant yeast
- 1 cup (240ml) warm water
- 2 tablespoons poppy seeds

Instructions:

Same as Kastenbrot, incorporating poppy seeds.

Walnussbrot (Walnut Bread)

Ingredients:

- 2 cups (250g) whole wheat flour
- 1 cup (125g) bread flour
- ½ cup (75g) chopped walnuts
- 1 teaspoon salt
- 1 teaspoon instant yeast
- 1 ¼ cups (300ml) warm water

Instructions:

Same as Kastenbrot, incorporating walnuts.

Quarkbrot (Quark Bread)

Ingredients:

- 2 cups (250g) bread flour
- 1 cup (250g) quark cheese
- 1 teaspoon salt
- 1 teaspoon instant yeast
- ½ cup (120ml) warm water

Instructions:

1. **Mix Dough:** Combine all ingredients, kneading into a soft dough.
2. **Knead:** Work dough for 10 minutes. Let rise for 1-2 hours.
3. **Shape:** Form into a loaf, let rise for 45 minutes.
4. **Bake:** Preheat oven to 375°F (190°C). Bake for 40-45 minutes.

Chia-Körnerbrot (Chia Seed Bread)

Ingredients:

- 2 cups (250g) whole wheat flour
- 1 cup (125g) bread flour
- 2 tablespoons chia seeds
- 1 teaspoon salt
- 1 teaspoon instant yeast
- 1 ¼ cups (300ml) warm water

Instructions:

Same as Kastenbrot, incorporating chia seeds.

Sauerteigbrot (Sourdough Bread)

Starter:

- 1 cup (120g) rye flour
- ½ cup (120ml) water
- ¼ teaspoon instant yeast

Dough:

- 2 cups (250g) rye flour
- 2 cups (250g) bread flour
- 1 ½ teaspoons salt
- 1 ¼ cups (300ml) warm water

Instructions:

1. **Starter Preparation:** Mix rye flour, water, and yeast. Let ferment for 8-12 hours.
2. **Dough Mixing:** Combine all ingredients, kneading into a soft dough.
3. **Knead:** Work dough for 10 minutes. Let rise for 2 hours.
4. **Shape:** Form into a round loaf, let rise for 1 hour.
5. **Bake:** Preheat oven to 450°F (230°C). Bake for 35-40 minutes.

Dinkelvollkornbrot (Whole Spelt Bread)

Ingredients:

- 3 cups (375g) whole spelt flour
- 1 teaspoon salt
- 1 teaspoon instant yeast
- 1 ¼ cups (300ml) warm water

Instructions:

Same as Kastenbrot, using whole spelt flour.

Hefezopf (Yeast Braid Bread)

Ingredients:

- 3 cups (375g) bread flour
- ¼ cup (50g) sugar
- 1 teaspoon salt
- 1 packet (7g) instant yeast
- ½ cup (120ml) warm milk
- ¼ cup (60g) butter, melted
- 1 egg
- 1 egg yolk + 1 tablespoon milk (for egg wash)

Instructions:

1. **Mix Dough:** Combine flour, sugar, salt, and yeast. Add warm milk, butter, and egg, kneading into a soft dough.
2. **Knead:** Work dough for 10 minutes. Let rise for 1-2 hours.
3. **Shape:** Divide into three strands, braid, and place on a baking sheet. Let rise for 45 minutes.
4. **Bake:** Preheat oven to 375°F (190°C). Brush with egg wash, bake for 25-30 minutes.

Rosinenbrot (Raisin Bread)

Ingredients:

- 3 cups (375g) bread flour
- ¼ cup (50g) sugar
- 1 teaspoon salt
- 1 teaspoon instant yeast
- ½ cup (120ml) warm milk
- ¼ cup (60g) butter, melted
- ½ cup (75g) raisins
- 1 egg

Instructions:

1. **Mix Dough:** Combine flour, sugar, salt, and yeast. Add warm milk, butter, raisins, and egg, mixing into a soft dough.
2. **Knead:** Work dough for 10 minutes. Let rise for 1-2 hours.
3. **Shape:** Form into a loaf, let rise for 45 minutes.
4. **Bake:** Preheat oven to 375°F (190°C). Bake for 40-45 minutes.

Nussbrot (Nut Bread)

Ingredients:

- 2 cups (250g) whole wheat flour
- 1 cup (125g) bread flour
- ½ cup (75g) chopped walnuts
- 1 teaspoon salt
- 1 teaspoon instant yeast
- 1 ¼ cups (300ml) warm water

Instructions:

Same as Rosinenbrot, incorporating walnuts.

Müsli-Brot (Muesli Bread)

Ingredients:

- 2 cups (250g) whole wheat flour
- 1 cup (125g) bread flour
- ½ cup (75g) mixed dried fruit
- ½ cup (50g) rolled oats
- ¼ cup (30g) chopped nuts
- 1 teaspoon salt
- 1 teaspoon instant yeast
- 1 ¼ cups (300ml) warm water

Instructions:

Same as Rosinenbrot, incorporating oats, dried fruit, and nuts.

Kastanienhonigbrot (Chestnut Honey Bread)

Ingredients:

- 2 cups (250g) bread flour
- 1 cup (150g) chestnut flour
- 1 teaspoon salt
- 1 teaspoon instant yeast
- 1 cup (240ml) warm water
- 2 tablespoons honey

Instructions:

Same as Rosinenbrot, incorporating chestnut flour and honey.

Apfelbrot (Apple Bread)

Ingredients:

- 2 cups (250g) bread flour
- 1 cup (250g) grated apples
- ¼ cup (50g) sugar
- 1 teaspoon cinnamon
- 1 teaspoon salt
- 1 teaspoon instant yeast
- ½ cup (120ml) warm milk

Instructions:

1. **Mix Dough:** Combine flour, sugar, cinnamon, salt, and yeast. Add grated apples and warm milk, mixing into a soft dough.
2. **Knead:** Work dough for 10 minutes. Let rise for 1-2 hours.
3. **Shape:** Form into a loaf, let rise for 45 minutes.
4. **Bake:** Preheat oven to 375°F (190°C). Bake for 40-45 minutes.

Kürbisbrot (Pumpkin Bread)

Ingredients:

- 2 cups (250g) bread flour
- 1 cup (250g) pumpkin purée
- ¼ cup (50g) sugar
- 1 teaspoon cinnamon
- 1 teaspoon salt
- 1 teaspoon instant yeast
- ½ cup (120ml) warm milk

Instructions:

Same as Apfelbrot, replacing apples with pumpkin purée.

Kirschenbrot (Cherry Bread)

Ingredients:

- 2 cups (250g) bread flour
- ½ cup (100g) dried or fresh cherries, chopped
- ¼ cup (50g) sugar
- 1 teaspoon salt
- 1 teaspoon instant yeast
- ½ cup (120ml) warm milk

Instructions:

Same as Apfelbrot, incorporating cherries.

Vanillebrot (Vanilla Bread)

Ingredients:

- 3 cups (375g) bread flour
- ¼ cup (50g) sugar
- 1 teaspoon vanilla extract
- 1 teaspoon salt
- 1 teaspoon instant yeast
- ½ cup (120ml) warm milk
- ¼ cup (60g) butter, melted

Instructions:

Same as Apfelbrot, incorporating vanilla extract.

Kokosbrot (Coconut Bread)

Ingredients:

- 2 cups (250g) bread flour
- ½ cup (50g) shredded coconut
- ¼ cup (50g) sugar
- 1 teaspoon salt
- 1 teaspoon instant yeast
- ½ cup (120ml) warm coconut milk

Instructions:

Same as Apfelbrot, incorporating shredded coconut and coconut milk.

Schokoladenbrot (Chocolate Bread)

Ingredients:

- 2 cups (250g) bread flour
- ¼ cup (25g) cocoa powder
- ½ cup (100g) chocolate chips
- ¼ cup (50g) sugar
- 1 teaspoon salt
- 1 teaspoon instant yeast
- ½ cup (120ml) warm milk

Instructions:

Same as Apfelbrot, incorporating cocoa powder and chocolate chips.

Früchtebrot (Fruit Bread)

Ingredients:

- 2 cups (250g) bread flour
- ½ cup (100g) mixed dried fruit
- ¼ cup (50g) sugar
- 1 teaspoon cinnamon
- 1 teaspoon salt
- 1 teaspoon instant yeast
- ½ cup (120ml) warm milk

Instructions:

Same as Apfelbrot, incorporating mixed dried fruit.

Maronenbrot (Marron Bread)

Ingredients:

- 2 cups (250g) bread flour
- 1 cup (150g) chestnut flour
- ¼ cup (50g) sugar
- 1 teaspoon salt
- 1 teaspoon instant yeast
- ½ cup (120ml) warm milk

Instructions:

Same as Apfelbrot, incorporating chestnut flour.

www.ingramcontent.com/pod-product-compliance
Lightning Source LLC
LaVergne TN
LVHW081506060526
838201LV00056BA/2964